# Elephant

## Rich Murphy

𝄢

**Bass Clef Books**
Cecilia, KY

First Edition

ISBN

979-8-9898478-5-3
$15.00

Bass Clef Books is an imprint of MARZEK Publishing
Mick Kennedy, Publisher

Printed and distributed by
Kindle Direct Publishing

# Table of Contents

# Showtime

(Too late) the mahout always arrives
after the subject enters the room
farming wall flowers against
a discreet wallpaper pattern.

A blind spot white noises,
stealing the oxygen from the hall,
short-leashing ears and voices
and goading inappropriate vocabulary
and silence with an ankus.

"Hey" and cocktail peanuts
show off controlled conversation
defining and framing discussion.

The sacred ground dance floor
cleared in four-four time
for an insistent trunk that lifts
through thin air assumption,
implication, and a driving argument.

The buzzing around the grey zone
articulates to ensure that flies
don't disturb sleeping acrobats
who don't forget language limits.

# Chronic Phonics

Tangled among media-fed frames
creative voices wrestle into knots
until punctuation and word
inventions overrun with images
and metaphors attempting
a closer resemblance.

Each match ends with language
pinned to frustrated four letters.

The unknowable chokes and twists
at every larynx effort to relax
in a mother whose tongue
marinated a lifetime in culture.

Poems and philosophical tracts
shave off bristling and dead skin
from neck, chin, and cheeks to drop
a wailing bundle on doorsteps
for a tomorrow free from phrases.

Each liminal Olympics hoped
for a lanky end to all linguistics
but limped away to cry again.

## Music Lesson

The circadian rhythm drums
with sun and moon monotony
that invites the What Now?
nervous system to rattle
ivories, cymbals, and senses.

After the trauma in arriving
between two legs, taught children
relax into lives without end
though know better than teachers
the dangers everywhere in fun.

Happy happy shines while
the syncopated selves shake
so that plates could fly from shelves
at any down beat from the young
adult suffering cognitive dissonance
between two experiences.

Tempering the internal questioning
with daily routine a life project
unto death in the practice room
could stretch into late style harmony.

# Experiencing the Light

Care beams with brilliance
from the sun into a joint-jittering
fuel tank until electrical charges
relay into a current project
for the past and future.

Few nerve bundles don't flee
from the invitation to live.
Decision, discipline, and death
race in hearts, trample clarity.
Palm screens sponge the sweat
from brows that become
lost to nature and selves.

When shaken, the bone bag
can grow from fear to concern
and spine, a strange human embrace
encouraging strategy for fulfillment.
Early examples reach out
and rescue with a lesson, look.

Once in the Hysterics Asylum
the happy hostage pays
for the getaway cell year
to year so that only nose steam
and rent receipts prove
to the animal kingdom
that a human roams Earth.

# Dopamine Dealers

Deeper into the airconditioned
nightmare ideology, cool business
tycoons discovered how to hack
habit against human life.
Better-tickle-promises comfort
when sweaty anxiety shines.

The drug pusher in the shade
and a three-piece suit whispers
to the unschooled young,
"Grow faster with this toy."

Parents juggling work, children,
and self-care flail with school
teachers in a Maybe Well in hand.
Mirror mirror show how to swim
between Charybdis and Scylla.

Cold turkey nerve-racks outside
the satellite and tower reach:
A fix, a fix, my family for a fix.
The open vein in the palm threatens
to bleed out in the marketplace.

# Who's a Mama?

The poor parenting epidemic
that wild-fires across countries
more and more today stems
from desperate topsoil
whether in well-to-do homes
or in a slum neighborhood.

The seeds and roots plant
in subpar sulfate mixed in
with bull and horse manure
during an information age
gone amuck with dopamine
and technology teasers.

Every small palm ignites
at schoolhouses to substitute
for nature walks, smelling roses,
and physical play outdoors.

An adult lost in a media
frensy drops behind to save
relationships while abandoning
the role of touchy feely living,
the grass in a sniff after rain.

Leaves and blossom wilt
in organic sadness while maybe
pleasure rewards this time.

# Network Net Worth

The ideology net drops
to snare spare time thinkers
and low information senses
that feed on how-to tidbits
and dropped line scraps
from social media.

Once in the halter-for-everyone
the burden beasts pull
around the dollar-making
machinery, an Egyptian
herd hauling pyramid blocks
to memorialize without the pain
but without consciousness either.

Without a pharaoh to bury,
homage to a collective
enslavement explores for wealth
with a blind spot around the world:
A planet annihilation.

Homo sapiens self-interest rolls
onward upon the bones and trees
from the wilderness, saving
the opposable thumb species for last.

# Habit Gauntlet

Lacking a morning problem
for the frontal lobe to chew on,
the transparent coping
with soap, water, and toweling
each day eats up a calendar square,
wolfing all meals on the fly.

The bologna sandwiches unto
the cemetery picnic pleads
at the originality altar
should the algorithmic morning
coffee not quake enough.

The ghost, a routine expert
arrives at the backdoor where
the idle car occupies the driveway
ready, but no mind at all.

The humdrummed hypnotized
nestle into another workday,
unless momentary glitches irritate
the wallet pocket or bead
anxiety on the forehead.

The evening couch catches the flop,
and television, where actors
by definition, fake it, balms,
no need for sleep.

# Permanence Pretense

Boilerplating into the future,
sweet spot and soul mate, exactitude,
go out the window and pant seats
determine when moving to marry
smarts with a halo.

Without fine tuning and adjusting
aims for effect a gingerbread regiment
marches through the streets cursing
the cookie cutter mentality
when pound cake may have been.

After all the problems within arms reach
have been roughed out and hammered,
sufferers continue to chew nails.

Templates rely on outer circles on a target
to cover the hit or miss peep sight bullseye.

The hack polishes for presentations
though a closer inspection confesses
to the lackluster record and promise
among garden-variety realtors.

Sore thumb blueprints and paradigms
shift from one reason to another
wearing bandanas while playing
tambourines and squeeze boxes.

# Through the Gates

A full-frontal assault on art
and audience by the all-behavior
economy ushes in the barbarism.

Painted into a corner each sunrise,
the time consumer, who wields thought
to craft paint, ink, sound,
slap dashes to professionalize on-the-go,
performing jig gigs around town.

Pick a partner and dose-doe for dough.

Pop up shop work here and there
to surprise loose change from pockets
or sleep in the rain with debtors,
the musician sings to the sun.

Every morning in a lifetime shows up
meaning business and nothing else
separating theft and an extra bow
from an image stamped on irises
and frontal lobes or else.

The beggar roles without Shakespeare
soothe with evidence consciences
in cars or on foot while setting off
the limbic warning spotlight

to throw together the never read
Prospero addictive illusion for signal
seekers who happen to pass by.

# Road Crew Heroes

Knitting a network with footsteps
and conversation to fish humans
from the deep digital blues, a bold salt
spidermans for a city face to each face.

Loneliness flits, lured into the worldwide
eye-to-eye web for lunch.
When anxiety serves up coffee,
the thread in small talk eases better than
antidepressants baited with gummies,
or a smoking habit reeling in the hooked.

A joyful belly-hello-bellow bounces
on a trampoline stretching each fret
and safety line that strum into music
for tambourine accompaniment and a smile.

The I-phone and laptop dupes,
the rented and surveilled ego herds,
get eaten up by the billions by fat men;
helpless futures in palms predict.

# Heart Throbbers

The gateway drug to heart health
activates when in the morning
on city streets housing has alleviated
the tented and boxed homes.

Before the entrance to the meaning
pumping culture, muscular squads
jump-and-jack, stretch in yoga
positions, and reach out handshakes,
hugs, and purpose invitations.

"Us and them" ruts into boredom:
Stalemate grows into stale mates.
So dopamine pusher man "yeh yehs"
into routine smiles a utopia punch line.

Applications to flesh freshen
with goodwill, "Butt Reality get off
the couch and build on memories
for jogging through a lifetime."

Introduction to hard stuff needle point
walks with kindness among people,
plants, and animals without Jones
keeping up influencers wedging.

## Staying Fresh

Playing odd ball in the schoolyard,
the beginner mind head scratches
at teachers all the way to graduation day.
"Each student can learn alone also."

The convention ignorant stands
alone in a commuter crowd,
not a fan around symbols and highways
but spots irony miles away
while tinkering and testing metaphors
all day long for best fits when given
new information to an imagination.

Happy with things as names seam
to situations and to objects
(common sense outside the window
and on television), the get-along-gang
moves along through life looking
forward to happily-ever-after, after all.

In living room indoors or outdoors,
Infant Terrible sits down to craft
a dictionary from Awe to Wonder
for each day for a lifetime.

# What a Big Box Stores

Once valued people had places to live,
banks iced the American Dream
somewhere near the North Pole.
Witnesses vouch that neighbor hoods
in ski masks dropped a concrete block
off a pier in the middle of the night.

Home building came to a crawl,
a beggar without a door for knocking on.
Laid off carpenters went to work
for refrigerator box manufacturers.

Setting down hammers and nails,
the roof-over-heads and chicken-
in-every-pot workers picked up
glue guns and folded cardboard
in factory lines for cold hearted
bosses who folded only fresh bills.

Before the make-shift housing production,
designers include for comfort enough
a corrugated bed and fresh air bath,
and the large mobile carton rests easily
on suburban and high rise
curbsides before trash day. Hurry!
The paper bungalow doubles as a coffin.

Should luck turn on a commuter,
the avenue sidewalk welcomes with beans
in a can and a spot to rest bones.

# The Fire Department

A spark that could ignite honesty
anywhere rings in at the ideology
alarm centers where greased poles
and ladder crews with print,
podcast, and AI firehoses dash
and splash in practice for dousing
and drowning light on a subject.

Twisted truths and bald-faced lies
wash down force-fed alternative facts
and drench swampy the sponges
between ears and behind eyeballs,
confusing clear thought on a sunny day.

The cynics race around the internet
spraying snide remarks subverting
hopeful attitudes and broad smiles.
Shouldered coping skills shrug.

Camouflaged among the misinformed,
the uncivil servants cussing and cursing,
and headline only multiple gigs worker,
an informed citizen stands in clown shoes.

# Blowing Bubbles

Bathtubs overflow with rumps,
bumps, and humps in some
countries while backwater
regions on the planet Earth
sip at anything that drips.

Embarrassing satellite images,
including naked privilege cover up,
expose when intercepted by pop
group Bubble Research and thrusted
by a dark room justice department
under noses that only accrue interest.

The television tube towels off
the cocooned spill masters
to keep the illusion thought
balloon afloat while the stick people
under a lack magnifier starve.

As guilt and shame find excuses,
concern and aid don't trickle down
into bellies and weak resentment dips
into self-blame, death shrouds
around one-by-one:
Not in sight not in mind.

# Pool Time

Wading through the empathy shallows,
the barefooted puddle splasher learns
from hearted shirt-sleeve cuffs
and crocodile tears fronting for the shadowy,
"Phew, that person remains less."

A social Darwinism scoreboard pins down
neighbors for the abuse for life.

Mutual respect sulks on the subconscious
bluff mumbling, "Hi Hope, at least
eye-to-eye doesn't call from a mountain peak."
Evolution may not climb to that height.

The supposed-to generations gatekeep
equal opportunity carrying a flimsy
definition while guarding rusty hinges
and permitting a fixed few through.

Only the stilted people pass, knowing
that the looking down behavior code
rules over squatters peering up.
The deep end, the deep blue, still.

# Hot Rod with Momentum

Reverse never existed on the shifter.
Miracles phooey into illusion.
Even "neutral" rolls forward though slowly.
The emergency brake conviction
lingers for the threatening loser only:
"No breaks" name tags stick.

All that pivoting when trying
to turn around shows off that evolution
navigates for the wise guy too.
Hot Rod souped-up a vehicle,
exhausting everyone in the neighborhood
while screeching and varooming.

Those traditional cultures seemingly
stuck in the mud spinning wheels
and churning curds may intuit
that mutants can carry a promise
in a million years if one could wait.

But an enlightened manic mechanic
gives up touring and mining landscapes
for the short cut: Driving curiosity
into the human resource and raw materials.

# Top-Down Weathering

Mechanics and engineers fell
from favor when the weather
overheated and climates began
breaking down just outside paradise.
The hardware reign dripped
into slick rainbow puddles
on busy city streets.

The prettiest girls slip through
greasy hands now, cooking up
futures to own alone: Barefoot
and aproned, the wench
left without a goodbye.

Wrenched from bed,
experts race into smog clouds
without a clue about where.
Useless foghorns and lighthouses
SOS to summon for icebreaker
help to assist locals in seeing
a lighthearted nature.

Close associates in lab coats
threw up hands after warning
half a century earlier, the needed
seed that went unheeded.

# Hurt Feelings Translator

Everyone knows at least a little Victimese.
Childhood often meets up with blunt
adulthood or natural tripping stone disasters.
The dead don't even speak in tongues,
so now lie cold-blooded and fluent.

The maimed and metaphorically maimed
claim to own the language and the country.
("Poor me") gets kicked around
in offices, homes, and on street corners.

In perfectly good English elite large targets
look for zingers from nonclass mates
and bullies because empathic benefits
also come with the slings and arrows
from the downtrodden and wounded.

Two countries over from a war zone,
names uttered or called out
face-to-face traumatize before dinner
where emotions for crying out loud
don't show up on the Richter scale.

# Bird Flu Inoculation Trials

At the school for eggshell walking,
every meal dishes out to students
omelets with toast and coffee,
no menu needed: No quiche.

"A" students tiptoe around dorms
and classrooms without a sound.
Scrambling jokes with serious silent
treatments, "C" settlers prep
for wise crack examinations on Fridays.

Practice becomes high-stepping live
when teachers tour en l'air across
campus, blackbirds with mortar boards,
when returning to touchy subjects
that raise bristles on pool balls
and fist for right and left wings.

Black-balled college presidents
and culture-canceled whole classes,
the once hard-boiled unity spills
into the streets and virtual alleyways
slipping up tongues, good thought,
and feet finding a way as a lark.

# Tourpreneur

The umbrella raises over
each grouping to prevent
diluting and drying out
kin in kind: Human limbs
and torso features, perhaps.

London or the beach weather
beats on the canvas, center pole,
and ribs that protect souvenirs
on shopping lists maybe.

The well organized
tour guides know that
the initiates fear
confusion found
under sun or rain.
A patient nail biter
can transform into
an ideal OCD patient.

Needing more than balance
and a highwire, the visiting
biped longs for a name,
a floor, a shelter, for example
in the hallway next to the door.

# Trouble Tending

Trouble tends to gather lenses
into a confusion, a cloud
that attracts other foggy
atmospheres and attitudes.

Funk lurks in legs and shoulders
with lows that apply pressure
on an otherwise good day.
A weatherman reports
that somewhere a star shines.

The blurring and dimming veils
until hands wring out lightning.
The new thunderhead
storms from aqua ducts,
along nose rivers, and into song:
"As blue as a boy can be" . . .
"When you haven't got a prayer"
Tissues issue for leaning into.

The sorting among glazes
gazes and shouts for adoption
by perspective, a friend,
a clearing to see through

A lifetime clique snaps into place
to ease the blind spot to come.

# Dogging a Diary

Each day a new chapter shelves
for the imaginary biographer
who reports in best light
on the victim and hero.

The ghostwriter with street creds
who crafts inside a human head
follows along taking notes
for cheering on the VIP:
A best friend without a leash.

At sundown, the saga leg
wears out the main character
while the spine never cracks
and not a single page turns:
A sad story, tragic really.

Worse yet, library cards
don't issue for readership
outside a novel body living.
Would-be book worms busy
relaying plots, excuses,
eyewitness accounts
for other private protagonists.

Dogear wishes wag tales
from Team Memoirist.

# Local Literature Developments

Where straining similes fall apart
and poles erect for totems, flags, and sails,
gurus self-select and saints
mutter from the grave:
Local populations die for metaphors.

Glue stick factory patrons pick up
the pieces for puzzling over
to reassure like or as in the living room.
Insistent identification projects
work with drum major magic
to unify the two-part promotion title, ThisThat.

From the thump thump knowing
by heart in time 3-D reasons
to stand firm without duct tape
emerge for knocking on for certainty,
a touchstone for reference letters:
Symbol cymbal crash, ta-da.

Language hardens into fortress walls
and soon into invasion tactics
and colonial strategies until the instigating
word tires into a loco cliché.

## Caruso, Starless

In the Utopian American states
colorful cultural capital
tucks under game board edges
in well-intentioned but empty
suburban rumpus rooms.

Minute meditators report.

Science orients and defines
for people pregnant with possibility
which means that technology
and sales navigate by blind desire
for a continent without a paddle.

Electric toothbrushes and migraine meds
buoy the bathroom mirror.

Homo sapiens children drop off
birthrate maps nudged by the treasured
wrong-headed ego that demands empathy.

Nihilist gurus and pop artists
cash in on reassurance agency.
The GPS arrives on Earth every time
for Western evolutionary deadenders.

Stranded among the latest Eden enviers,
the space traveler wonders only.

# Communique

Bodies shelve in books
to animate character and spirits
that shelve books in bodies.

Vicarious libraries walk
around as unsuspecting historians
for emulating should an empty
drum dub, dumb, dumb.

Ancient heroic deeds
and daily habits and vital forgotten
behavior pull from the sapiens
torsos lessons in human practice.

These days the footbridge
between yesterday and tomorrow
stages for a momentary unrecorded
common ground performance.

Take a selfie each day for a lifetime:
Flash for whom, about what?
beyond instinct made banal. Blink.

# Factor Backdoor

The tour sign read as follows:
"Welcome to the Banality Factory
(where the assembly line works
the streets joking about evil and the root)."

Any teen can sleep through
the ins and outs that last a lifetime.
Critical thinking skills rest unused
on bomb shelter dust collection shelves.
That lever for everyday psyche pressure
jargons into platitudes and clichés:
Work-around, silver lining, buzzword.

When some brat feeds the conveyor
with the most outrageous sensation
(xual revolution, for example),
and includes raw news footage
that tickles gun grabber panic buttons,
desublimation firehoses will splash
across faces watching on screens
and earworm deep into whorls
for good measure until respectable citizens
cha-ching the goods from the Dollar Store.

# Spell

Under a language trance
zombies perform for culture
with touchy feely reassurance:
Nose tweaking strangers
while with palms plowing
to the roadside foreign gibberish.

A wand spells out the terms.
Poof! A sentence detours,
copping until a cliff waves on
into a ravine: dead end deft
to a platitude attitude.

Any person outside dialect
groupings need not apply.
Translation bends into a head
scratching dumb found dub.

The human toolbox opens to:
Index fingers point for the tongue
and opposable thumbs hold
onto the pencil with eraser.

# Deuces Wild

Frightened into language and culture
each species member poker-faces
into believing this means, that means.
Sceptics jibber-jabber only.

At the card table also, the bluff caller
dresses as a dupe, naïve to the intricate
shuffles, deals, hands, and tricks
that draw from the bottom in the deck.

Embedded in a "hit me" society
that best bets, a maverick and a straight
man sport the look that opens doors
to health and some wealth too.

With game on for the sharks and jokers,
the dumb all-in poet wearing jester hat
sees, raises, and slights, stealing
words from tongues and ears.

The moment that stuns quiet, studs
with the return to the primal experience
from the noise that points.

# Acknowledgements

"Heart Throbbers" *Sein und Werden*

"What a Big Box Stores," "Road Crew Heroes," Blowing Bubbles," "Pool Time," and "Staying Fresh" *BlazeVOX*

# About the Author

Rich Murphy's poetry has appeared in *North Dakota Quarterly, Experiential-Experimental-Literature* (Ukraine), *Terror House Magazine* (Hungary), *Otoliths* (Australia), *Die Leere Mitte* (Germany), *Bangalore Review* (India), Lit. 202 (England), Calameo, *The Ofi Press* (Mexico), *Sein und Werden* (UK), *Neologism Poetry Journal, Word for / Word, Review Americana, West Texas Literary Review, New Note Poetry Journal, Grey Sparrow, Last Stanza Poetry Journal, Chiron Review, Flatbush Review,* and *Fractured Ecologies* (anthology, Denmark). *Prophet Voice Now* his book-length collection of essays on poetry and poetics was a finalist in the book contest at Common Ground Research Network and published in June 2020.